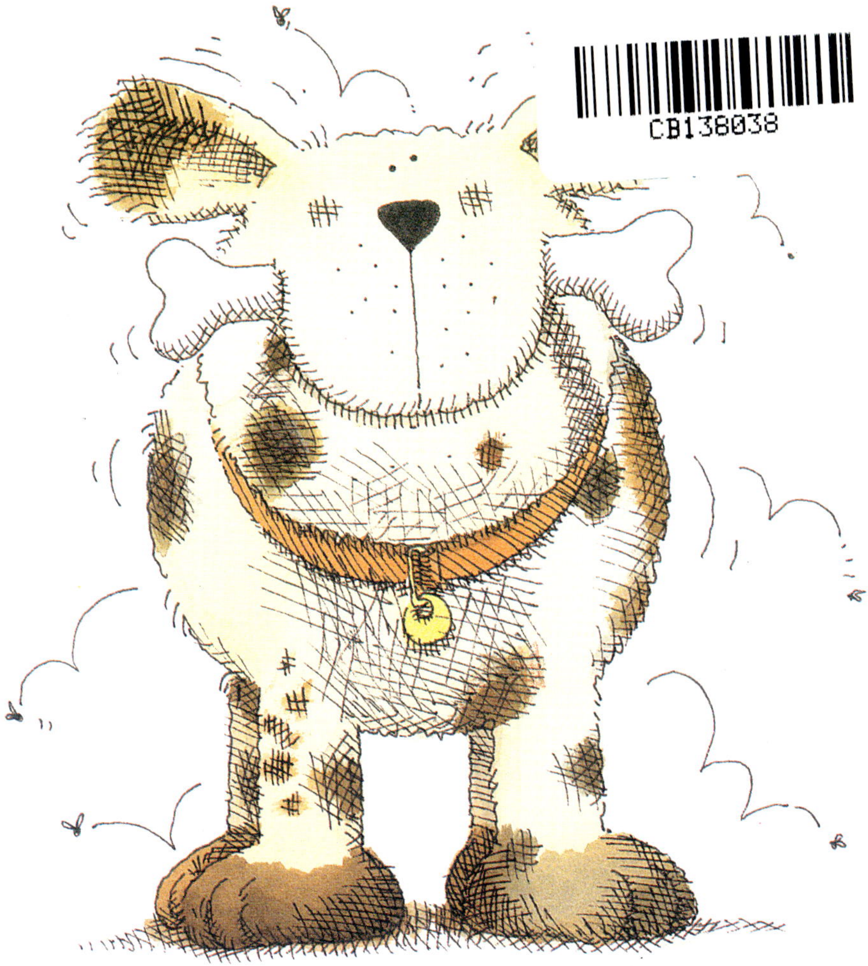

When my dog is dirty,

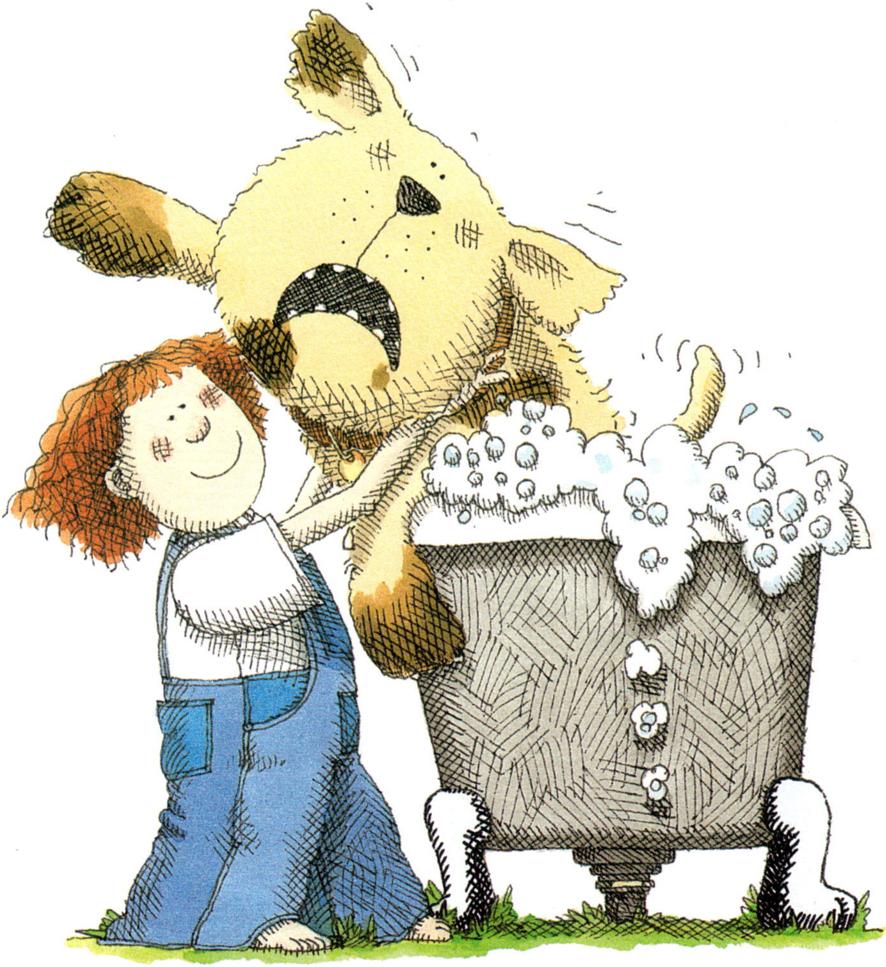

I give her a bath.

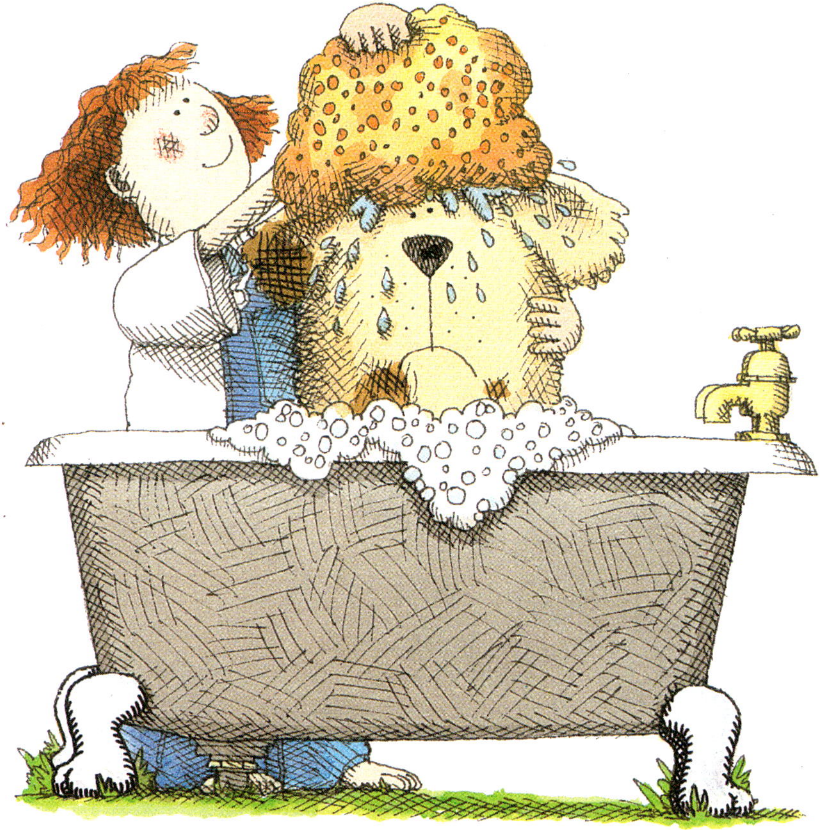

First I wet her,

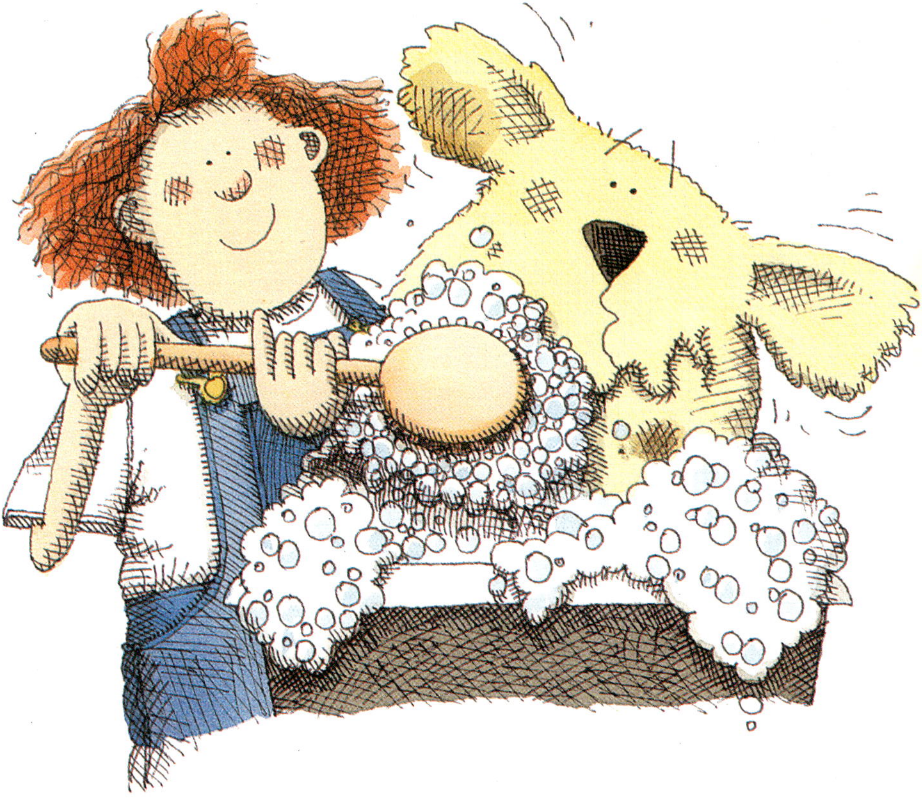

then I wash her.

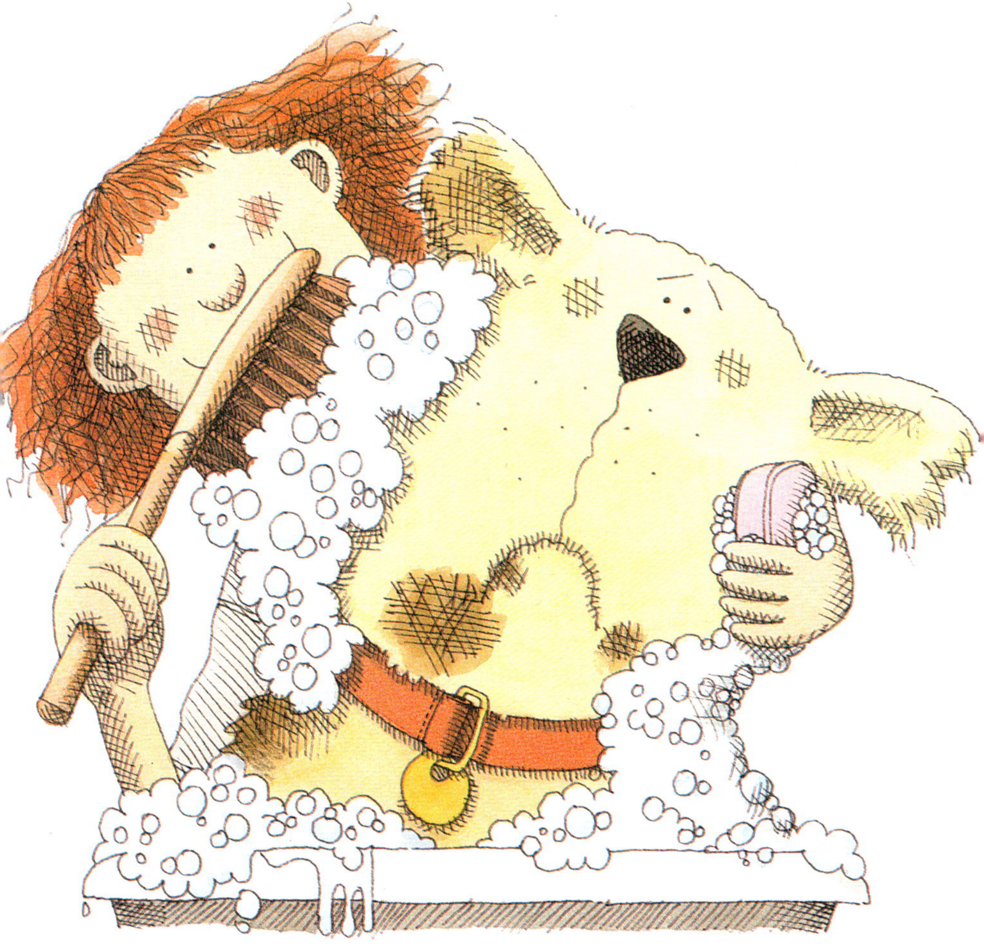

She doesn't like it!

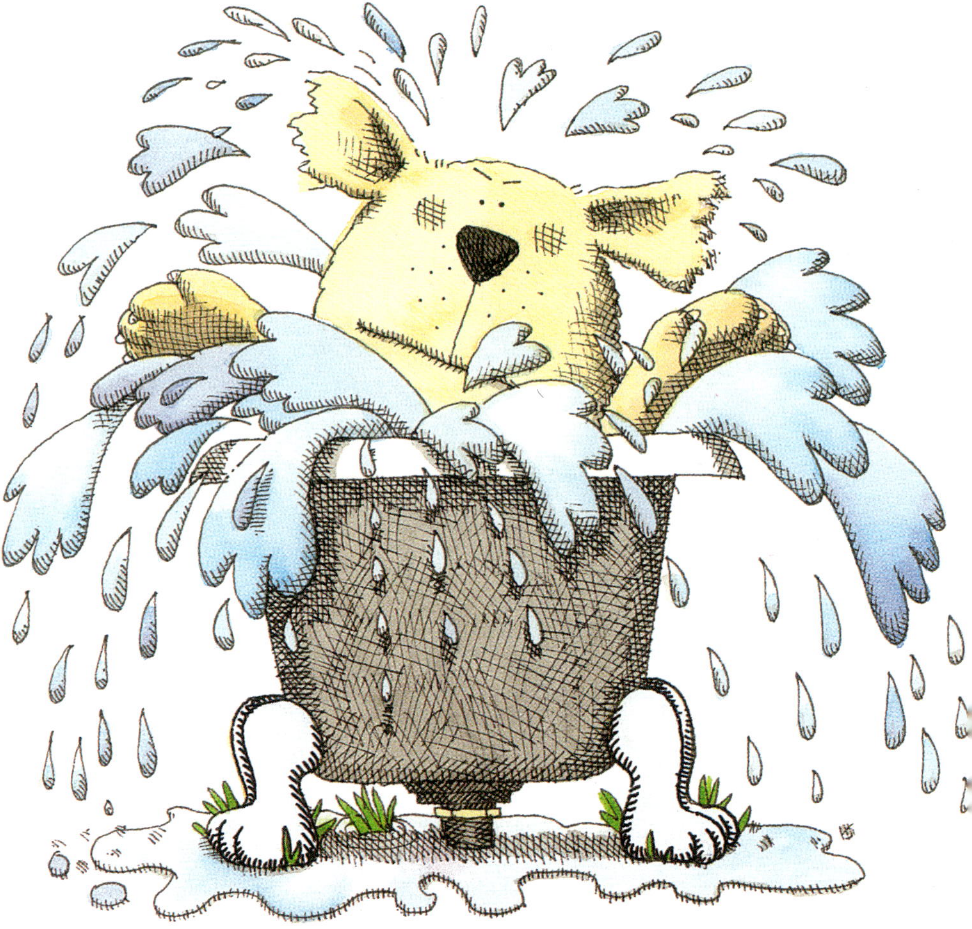

She kicks and she splashes.

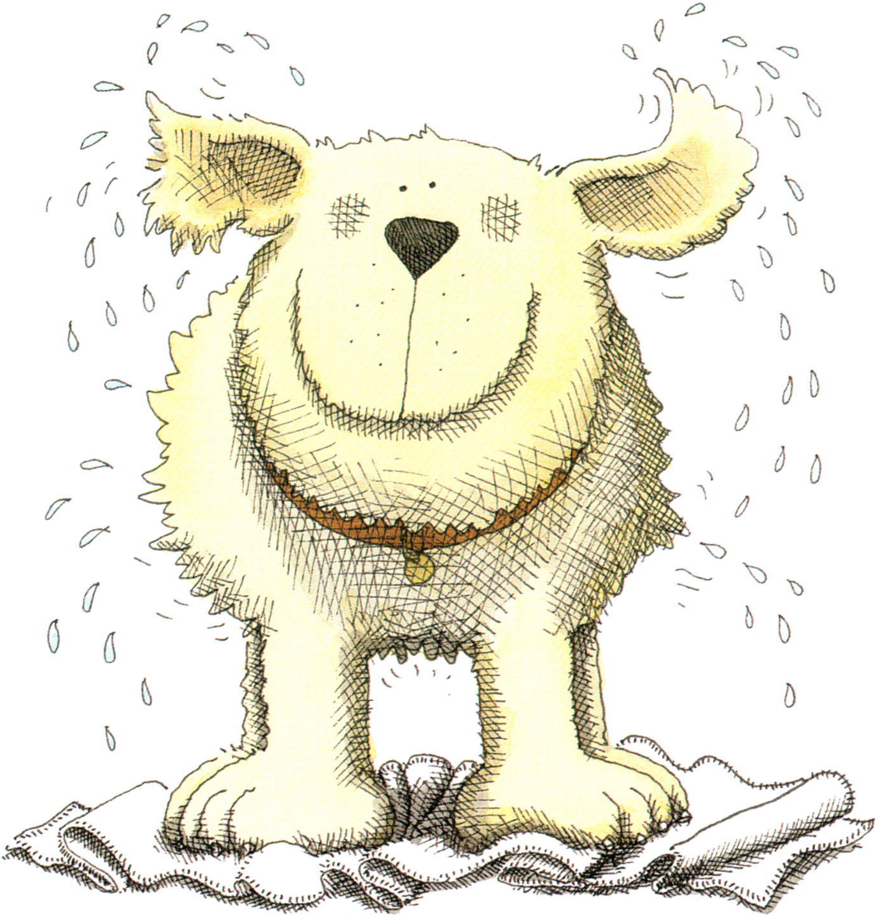

My dog is nice and clean now.

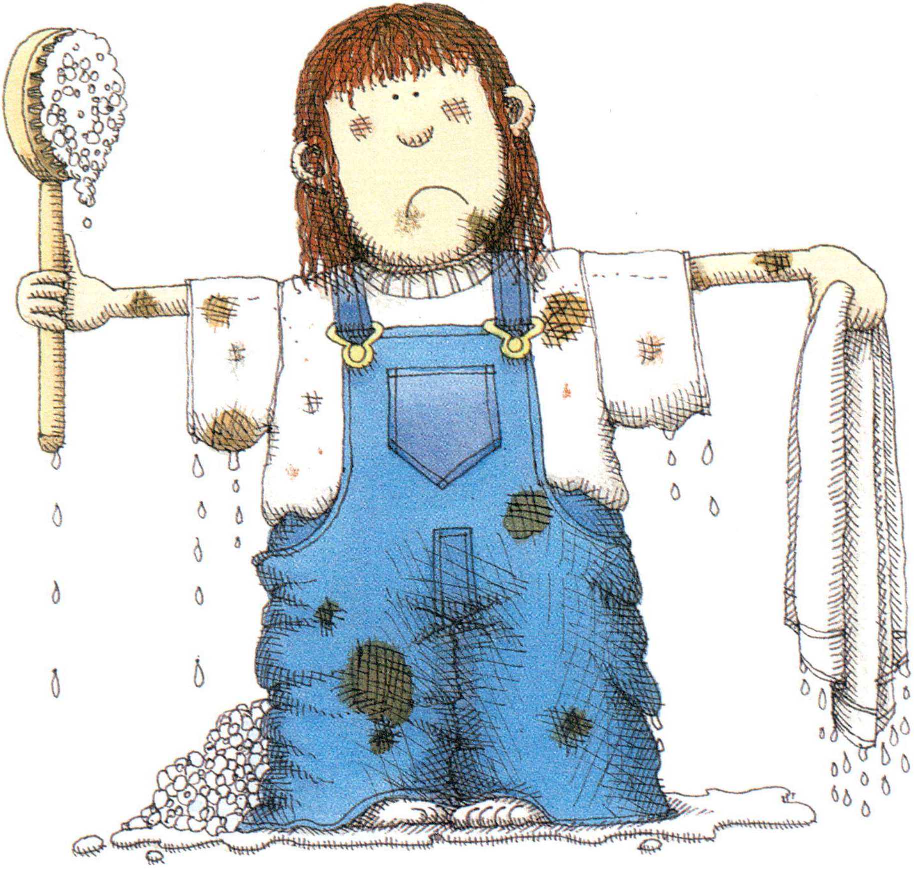

But look at me!